Why I Am Not a Christian

Four Conclusive Reasons to Reject the Faith

by

Richard Carrier, Ph.D.

Philosophy

2011

To truth, reason,
and common sense.

Why I Am Not a Christian:
Four Conclusive Reasons to Reject the Faith
Copyright © 2011 by Richard Carrier, Ph.D.
All Rights Reserved

Published by Philosophy Press
(Richmond, California)

www.richardcarrier.info

1. Free thought.
2. Christianity—Criticism, interpretation, etc.

ISBN: 978-1456588854

Contents

Why This Book

I'm cognitively defective. Or that's what Christians tell me. It's not true, of course. But the curious thing is how desperately they need to believe there is something wrong with me. For otherwise, they cannot explain how someone so well informed about their religion could reject their faith—indeed, someone who doesn't just give it a pass, but rejects it as firmly as any other bizarre cult or superstition. Which is what it is. This book is about why.

Once upon a time, a generous fellow by the name of John Ransom hired me to write out my reasons for rejecting the Christian religion. The result was an online essay, of which this is an updated edition in print. Why a print edition? Because yet another generous fellow wanted there to be one. So he arranged for this book to be published. "It's just too important, too well put, not to have it in a handy carry-about form," he said. In this way we can take it with us, store it on our shelves (or in our kindles), read it while all cozy on our couches or

1

lawns, write notes in the margins, hand copies out to other people willing to read it. Besides, he said, Christian fundamentalists need something to burn at the next Nuremburg rally.

Why me? Well, I've become something of a world renowned atheist, noted for my work in both history and philosophy, particularly in my criticism of the dubious and often delusional claims of various Christians. Just google my name and you'll see what I mean. Given my close study of the issues and my renown for cutting straight to the heart of them, I should summarize my case, John said, simply and clearly so everyone can understand where I'm coming from. He was especially frustrated by Christians who routinely come up with implausible excuses to defend their faith, which they don't really examine—as if defending their faith with any excuse mattered more than having a genuinely good reason to believe in the first place.

Discussing our experiences, we realized we'd both encountered many Christians like this, who color their entire perception of reality with the assumption that they *have* to be right, and therefore the evidence must somehow fit. So they think they can make anything up on the spur of the moment and be "sure" it's true. This is the exact opposite of what *we* do. We start with the evidence, and then figure out what the best explanation of it all really is, regardless of where this quest for truth takes us. John and I also shared the same experiences in another respect: when their dogmatism meets our empiricism, slander is not far behind. I have increasingly encountered Christians who accuse me to my face of being a liar, of being wicked, of not wanting to talk to God, of willfully ignoring evidence, of being "cognitively defective"—because that is the only way they can explain my existence. I cannot be an honest, well-informed pursuer of the truth who came to a fair and reasonable decision after a thorough examination of the evidence, because no such person can exist in the Christian worldview, who does not come to Christ. Therefore, I *must* be a wicked liar, I *must* be so deluded by sin that I am all but clinically insane, an irrational madman suffering some evil demonic psychosis.

There is nothing I can do for such people. Nothing I ever show or say to them will ever convince them otherwise—it *can't*, because they start with the assumption that their belief in Christ *has* to be true, therefore *right from the start* everything I say or do is always going to be a lie or the product of some delusion. They don't need any evidence of this, because to their thinking it *must* be the case. Such people are trapped in their own hall of mirrors, and for them there is no escape. They can never know whether they are wrong, even when they are. No evidence, no logic, no reason will ever get through to them.

When we combine this troubling fact with the observation that their religion, like every other, appears tailor-made to justify their own culture-bound desires and personal vanities—as if every God is made in man's image, not the other way around—then we already have grounds for suspicion. The fact that the Christian idea of God has constantly changed to suit our cultural and historical circumstances, and is often constructed to be impervious to logic or doubt, is reason enough to step back and ask ourselves whether we're on the wrong track with the Christian worldview. And the fact that Christianity is identical in all these respects to *other* religions—like Hinduism or Islam, which every Christian must agree are false faiths yet are nevertheless just as firmly believed, on essentially the same force of evidence, and defended with essentially the same excuses—should finally shake anyone out of their complacency and compel them to ask whether they, too, are as blind as all those other people with false religions. But anyone who is not thus shaken will be incapable of ever knowing who is wrong...is it those people, or themselves?

This essay will never convince Christians who have locked themselves inside a box of blind faith like this. But for other Christians out there who actually have an open mind, a good summary of my reasons for rejecting Christianity will help show why I am not a deluded liar, but in fact an honest and reasonable man coming to an honest and reasonable decision. What follows is not meant to be a thorough exploration of every nuance and problem, nor an exhaustive account of all the arguments and evidence. Rather, it's a mere summary of the four most important reasons I am not a Christian. This is only the beginning of the story, not the whole of it. That's what my benefactor asked for: a simple but well-written explanation of why I am not a Christian.

If you need more, if you want to see how I got here from close and extensive study of the relevant facts, both historical and philosophical, then I have a large body of work out there for you to explore. Start with my books **Sense and Goodness without God** (2005) and **Not the Impossible Faith** (2009), and my chapters in John Loftus' book **The End of Christianity** (2011). My work on the historical evidence of Jesus' resurrection appears in Loftus' earlier book **The Christian Delusion** (2010) and Lowder & Price's book **The Empty Tomb: Jesus Beyond the Grave** (2005). More can be found through my website: **richardcarrier.info**.

For the present book I shall assume that C.S. Lewis was correct when he said "mere Christianity" consisted in the belief that "there is one God" who "is quite definitely good or righteous," "who takes sides, who loves love and hates hatred, who wants us to behave in one way and not in another," and who "invented and made the universe." But this God also "thinks that a great many things have gone wrong" with the world and thus "insists, and insists very loudly, on our putting them right again," and to this end he arranged the death and resurrection of "His only Son," Jesus Christ, who is (or embodies or represents) the Creator, and can alone "save" us from "eternal death" if we now ask this Jesus to forgive our sins. That's as quoted and paraphrased from his aptly titled (and very popular) tract *Mere Christianity*.

If this is what Christianity is (and most Christians appear to believe so), then there are four reasons why I do not believe a word of it. And all four would have to be answered with a clear preponderance of evidence before I would ever change my mind. I'm serious about this, too. If all four points are ever refuted with solid, objective evidence, then any other quibbles I have beyond these four would not stop me from declaring faith in Christ. For surely any other problem I or anyone might find with the Christian worldview could easily be solved from within the faith itself—if it weren't for the following four facts. So to those we now turn.

God is Silent

If God wants something from me, he would tell me. He wouldn't leave someone else to do this, as if an infinite being were short on time. And he would certainly not leave fallible, sinful humans to deliver an endless plethora of confused and contradictory messages. God would deliver the message himself, directly, to each and every one of us, and with such clarity as the most brilliant being in the universe could accomplish. We would all hear him out and shout "Eureka!" So obvious and well-demonstrated would his message be. It would be spoken to each of us in exactly those terms we each would understand. And we would all agree on what that message was. Even if we rejected it, we would all at least admit to each other, "Yes, that's what this God fellow told me." I came to this conclusion on my own, from obvious common sense, but it has been thoroughly demonstrated by renowned philosophers as well: see J.L. Schellenberg's *Divine Hiddenness and Human Reason* (1993) as well as Ted Drange's *Nonbelief and Evil* (1998) and Nicholas Everitt's *The Non-Existence of God* (2003).

Excuses don't fly. The Christian proposes that a supremely powerful being exists who *wants* us to set things right, and therefore *doesn't* want us to get things even more wrong. This is certainly an intelligible hypothesis, which predicts there should be no more confusion about which religion or doctrine is true than there is about the fundamentals of medicine, engineering, physics, chemistry, or even meteorology. It should be indisputably clear what God wants us to do, and what he doesn't want us to do. Any disputes that might still arise about that would be as easily and decisively resolved as any dispute between two doctors, chemists, or engineers as to the right course to follow in curing a patient, identifying a chemical, or designing a bridge. Yet this is not what we observe. Instead, we observe exactly the opposite: unresolvable disagreement and confusion. That is clearly a failed prediction. A failed prediction means a false theory. Therefore, Christianity is false.

Typically, Christians try to make excuses for God that "protect our free will." Either the human will is more powerful than the will of God, and therefore can actually block his words from being heard despite all his best and mighty efforts, or God cares more about our free choice not to hear him than about saving our souls, and so God himself "chooses" to be silent. Of course, there is no independent evidence of either this remarkable human power to thwart God *or* this peculiar desire in God, and so this is a completely *ad hoc* theory: something just "made up" out of thin air in order to

8

rescue the actual theory that continually fails to fit the evidence. But for reasons I'll explore in a later chapter, such "added elements" are never worthy of belief unless independently confirmed: you have to *know* they are true. You can't just "claim" they are true. Truth is not invented. It can only be discovered. Otherwise, Christianity is just a hypothesis that has yet to find sufficient confirmation in actual evidence. And no such hypothesis should be believed in, until that required evidence appears.

Be that as it may. Though "maybe, therefore probably" is not a logical way to arrive at any belief, let's assume the Christian can somehow "prove" (with objective evidence everyone can agree is relevant and true) that we have this power or God has this desire. Even on that presumption, there are unsolvable problems with this "additional" hypothesis. Right from the start, it fails to explain why *believers* disagree. The fact that believers can't agree on the content of God's message or desires also refutes the theory that he wants us to be clear on these things. This failed prediction cannot be explained away by any appeal to free will— for these people *have* chosen to hear God, and not only to hear him, but to accept Jesus Christ as the shepherd of their very soul. So no one can claim these people chose not to hear God. Therefore, either God is telling them different things, or there is no Christian God. Those are the only options left. Yet if there is a God who is deliberately sowing confusion, this contradicts what Christianity predicts to be God's desire, which entails Christianity is the wrong religion. And if God *isn't* telling his willing believers different things, then he isn't telling them anything, which *also* contradicts what Christianity predicts to be God's desire, which also entails Christianity is the wrong religion. So either way, Christianity is false.

So this excuse doesn't work. It fails to predict what we actually observe. You might still insist "I hear God!" But do you? How is your "inner voice of God" any more God's actual voice than a Muslim's or a Hindu's or a Catholic's or a Mormon's or a Luheran's or a Calvinist's? Or anyone else's? God is either sowing confusion (or allowing it to be sowed), and therefore in no way the Christian God, or none of you are hearing God, but just your own inner voice, which you have mistaken for God's (and if *they* all make this mistake, so can you). Which the Christian God would never in good conscience allow. So again, there can be no Christian God.

You can't escape this by claiming we have to persuade ourselves that God exists before we can hear him, for that's the very method of self-delusion that produces this result: universal disagreement and confusion over what God is actually saying. God would never require you to deploy a method "to know him" that demonstrably leads everyone else into error, because he would know that you would know (or would someday discover) that this proves such a method is wholly unreliable. A loving God would demand instead a method actually capable of distinguishing the true God from

false. Which means if this self-persuasion is the
only method you know, then there is no *God* who
cares whether you get it right, but only a *method* of
deluding yourself into believing there is—the very
same method by which everyone else (Muslim,
Hindu, Moonie, Mormon, Calvinist) is as deluded
as you.

That follows just from observing the confusion and disagreement of willing believers. But
even considering atheists like me, this *ad hoc* excuse for God's silence still fails to save Christianity
from the evidence. When I doubted the Big Bang
theory, I voiced the reasons for my doubts but con-
tinued to pursue the evidence, frequently speaking
with several physicists who were "believers."
Eventually, they presented all the logic and evidence in terms I understood, and I realized I was
wrong: the Big Bang theory *is* well-supported by
the evidence and is at present the best explanation
of all the facts by far. Did these physicists violate
my free will? Certainly not. I chose to pursue the
truth and hear them out. So, too, I and countless
others have chosen to give God a fair hearing—if
only he would speak. I would listen to him even
now, at this very moment. Yet he remains silent.
Therefore, it cannot be claimed that I am "choosing" not to hear him. And therefore, the fact that he
still does not speak refutes the hypothesis. Nothing
about free will can save the theory here. Christianity is simply refuted by the plain facts.

Even when we might actually credit free will
with resisting God's voice—like the occasional ir-

rational atheist, or the stubbornly mistaken theist—Christianity is *still* not compatible with the premise that God would not or could not overcome this resistance. Essential to the Christian hypothesis, as C.S. Lewis says, is the proposition that God is "quite definitely good" and "loves love and hates hatred." Unless these statements are completely meaningless, they entail that God would behave like anyone else who is "quite definitely good" and "loves love and hates hatred." And such people don't give up on someone until their resistance becomes intolerable—until then, they will readily violate someone's free will to save them, because they know darned well it's the right thing to do. God would do the same. He would not let the choice of a fallible, imperfect being thwart his own good will.

I know this for a fact. Back in my days as a flight-deck firefighter, when our ship's helicopter was on rescue missions, we had to stand around in our gear in case of a crash. There was usually very little to do, so we told stories. One I heard was about a rescue swimmer. She had to pull a family out of the water from a capsized boat, but by the time the chopper got there, it appeared everyone had drowned except the mother, who was for that reason shedding her life vest and trying to drown herself. The swimmer dove in to rescue her, but the woman kicked and screamed and yelled to let her die. She even gave the swimmer a whopping black eye. But the swimmer said to hell with that, I'm bringing you in! And she did, enduring her curses and blows all the way.

Later, it turned out that one of the victim's children, her daughter, had survived. She had drifted pretty far from the wreck, but the rescue team pulled her out, and the woman who had beaten the crap out of her rescuer apologized and thanked the swimmer for saving her against her will. Everyone in my group agreed the rescue swimmer had done the right thing, and we all would have done the same—because that is what a loving, caring being does. It follows that if God is a loving being, he will do no less for us. In the real world, kind people don't act like some stubborn, pouting God who abandons the drowning simply because they don't want to be helped. They act like this rescue swimmer. They act like us.

So we can be certain God would make sure he told everyone, directly, what his message was. Everyone would then know what God had told them. They can still reject it all they want, and God can leave them alone. Their free will remains. But there would never be, in any possible Christian universe, any confusion or doubt as to *what God's message was*. And if we had questions, God himself would answer them—just like the Big Bang physicists who were so patient with me. Indeed, the very fact that God gave the same message and answers to everyone would be nearly insurmountable proof that Christianity was true. Provided we had no reason to suspect God of lying to all of us, Christianity would be as certain as the law of grav-

Why I Am Not a Christian

ity or the color of the sky. That is what the Christian hypothesis entails we should observe—for it is what a good and loving God would do, who wanted us all to set right what has gone wrong. And since this is not what we observe, but in fact the exact opposite, the evidence quite soundly refutes Christianity.

Despite this conclusion, Christians still try to hold on to their faith with this nonsense about free will—but they haven't thought it through. Meteorologists can disagree about the weather forecast, but they all agree how weather is made and the conditions that are required for each kind of weather to arise. And they agree about this because the scientific evidence is so vast and secure that it resolves these questions, often decisively. It can't be claimed that God has violated the free will of meteorologists by providing them with all this evidence. And yet how much more important is salvation than the physics of weather! If God wants what Christianity says he wants, he would not violate our free will to educate us on the trivial and then refuse to do the same for the most important subject of all. Likewise, if a doctor *wants* a patient to get well, he is not vague about how he must do this, but as clear as can be. He explains what is needed in terms the patient can understand. He even answers the patient's questions, and whenever asked will present all the evidence for and against the effectiveness of the treatment. He won't hold anything back and declare, "I'm not going to tell you, because that would violate your free will!"

Nor would any patient accept such an excuse—to the contrary, he would respond, "But I *choose* to hear you," leaving the doctor no such excuse.

There can't be any excuse for God, either. There are always disagreements, and there are always people who don't follow what they are told or what they know to be true. But that doesn't matter. Chemists all agree on the fundamental facts of chemistry. Doctors all agree on the fundamental facts of medicine. Engineers all agree on the fundamental facts of engineering. So why can't all humans agree on the fundamental facts of salvation? There is no more reason that they should be confused or in the dark about this than that chemists, doctors, and engineers should be confused or in the dark.

The logically inevitable fact is, if the Christian God existed, we would all *hear from God himself* the same message of salvation, and we would all hear, straight from God, all the same answers to all the same questions. The Chinese would have heard it. The Native Americans would have heard it. Everyone today, everywhere on Earth, would be hearing it, and their records would show everyone else in history had heard it, too. Sure, maybe some of us would still balk or reject that message. But we would still have the information. Because the only way to make an informed choice is to have the required information. So a God who wanted us to make an informed choice would give us all the information we needed, and not entrust fallible, sinful, contradictory agents to convey a confused mess of ambiguous, poorly supported claims. Therefore, the fact that God hasn't spoken to us directly, and hasn't given us all the same, clear message, and the same, clear answers, is enough to prove Christianity false.

Just look at what Christians are saying. They routinely claim that God is your father and best friend. Yet if that were true, we would observe all the same behaviors from God that we observe from our fathers and friends. But we don't observe this. Therefore, there is no God who is our father or our friend. The logic of this is truly unassailable, and no "free will" excuse can escape it. For my father and friends aren't violating my free will when they speak to me, help me, give me advice, and answer my questions. Therefore, God would not violate my free will if *he* did so. He must be able to do at least as much as they do, even if for some reason he couldn't do more. But God doesn't do *anything at all*. He doesn't talk to, teach, help, or comfort us, unlike my real father and my real friends. God doesn't tell us when we hold a mistaken belief that shall hurt us. But my father does, and my friends do. Therefore, no God exists who is even remotely like my father or my friends, or anyone at all who loves me. Therefore, Christianity is false.

The conclusion is inescapable. If Christianity were true, then the Gospel would have been preached to each and every one of us directly, and correctly, by God—just as it supposedly was to the disciples who walked and talked and dined with God Himself, or to the Apostle Paul, who claimed to have had actual conversations with God, and to have heard the Gospel directly from God Himself. Was their free will violated? Of course not. Nor would ours be. Thus, if Christianity were really true, there would be no dispute as to what the Gospel *is*. There would only be our free and informed choice to accept or reject it. At the same time, all our sincere questions would be answered by God, kindly and clearly, and when we compared notes, we would find that the Voice of God gave consistent answers and messages to everyone all over the world, all the time. So if Christianity were true, there would be no point in "choosing" whether God exists anymore than there is a choice whether gravity exists or whether all those other people exist whom we love or hate or help or hurt. We would not face any choice to believe on insufficient and ambiguous evidence, but would know the facts, and face only the choice whether to love and accept the God that does exist. That this is not the reality, yet it would be the reality if Christianity were true, is conclusive proof that Christianity is false.

God is Inert

The God proposed by the Christian hypothesis is not a disembodied, powerless voice whose only means of achieving his desires is speaking to people, teaching them to do what's right. The Christian God is an Almighty Creator, capable of creating or destroying anything, capable of suspending or rewriting the laws of nature, capable of anything we can imagine. He can certainly do any and every moral thing you or I can do, and certainly much more than that, being so much bigger and stronger and better than we are in every way. All this follows necessarily from the definition of even "mere" Christianity, and therefore cannot be denied without denying Christianity itself.

It's a simple fact of direct observation that if *I* had the means and the power, and could not be harmed for my efforts, I would immediately alleviate all needless suffering in the universe. All guns and bombs would turn to flowers. All garbage dumps would become gardens. There would be adequate resources for everyone. There would be no more children conceived than the community and the environment could support. There would be no need of fatal or debilitating diseases or birth defects, no destructive Acts of God. And whenever men and women seemed near to violence, I would intervene and kindly endeavor to help them peacefully resolve their differences. That's what any loving person would do. Yet I cannot be more loving, more benevolent than the Christian God. Therefore, the fact that the Christian God does none of these things—in fact, nothing of any sort whatsoever—is proof positive that there is no Christian God.

If God at least did *something*, however much we might still argue about what that action meant about his ability, character, and desires, we would at least have evidence (and therefore reason to believe) that a God existed, maybe even the Christian God. And there are many things any god could do. He could make all true bibles indestructible, unalterable, and self-translating. He could make miraculous healing or other supernatural powers so common an attribute of the virtuous believer that they would be scientifically studied and confirmed as surely as any other medicine or technology. Hospitals would even have *bona fide* "faith healing" wings. As I explained in the previous chapter, he could speak to all of us in the same voice, saying the same things. Or he could send angels to appear to us on a regular basis, performing all manner of divine deeds and communications—exactly as the earliest Christians thought he did.

The possible evidences a God could provide are endless, though none might be sufficient to prove we have the Christian God. To prove *that*, this evident God would have to act as the Christian hypothesis predicts. For example, only those who believe in the true Christian Gospel would be granted the supernatural powers that would be confirmed by science; only true Christian Bibles would be indestructible, unalterable, and self-translating; and the Divine Voice would consistently convey to everyone the will and desires of the Christian message alone. But God does none of these things—nothing at all.

A Christian can rightly claim he is unable to predict *exactly* what things his God would choose to do. But the Christian hypothesis still entails that God would do *something*. Therefore, the fact that God does *nothing* is a decisive refutation of the Christian hypothesis. Once again a prediction is made that consistently fails to pan out. Instead, we observe the exact opposite: a dumb, mechanical universe that blindly treats everyone with the same random fortune and tragedy regardless of merit or purpose. But that's a fact we'll examine in a later chapter. For now, it's enough to note that we do not observe God doing good deeds, therefore there is no God who can or wants to do good deeds—which means Christianity is false.

Excuses won't fly here, either, because a loving being by definition acts like a loving being. It is a direct contradiction to claim that someone is loving yet never does what a loving person does—because the name refers to the behavior. To be loving literally means to *be* loving. You can't be heartless and claim to be loving. As Christ himself is supposed to have said, "it is by their fruits that shall ye know them." The only possible exception here is when a loving person is *incapable* of acting as he desires—either lacking the ability or facing too great a risk to himself or others—but this exception never applies to a God, who is all-powerful and immune to all harm. This exception never even applies to any human so absolutely that she can *never* act loving. Even the most limited and constrained person there is can at least do *something* that expresses their loving nature. Indeed, if it were ever truly possible to completely prevent this, a truly loving person would probably prefer death to such a horrible existence. And a loving God would be no different. Failing to act in a loving way would be unbearable for a loving being. There is no escaping the conclusion. From having the desire and the means to act in a loving way, it follows necessarily that God would so act. But he doesn't. Therefore, once again, the Christian God does not exist.

Think about it. A man approaches a school with a loaded assault rifle, intent on mass slaughter. A loving person speaks to him, attempts to help him resolve his problems or to persuade him to stop, and failing that, punches him right in the kisser, and takes away his gun. And a loving person with godlike powers could simply turn his bullets into popcorn as they left the gun, or heal with a touch whatever insanity or madness (or by teaching him cure whatever ignorance) led the man to contemplate the crime. But God does nothing. Therefore, a loving God does not exist. A tsunami approaches and will soon devastate the lives of millions. A loving person warns them, and tells them how best to protect themselves and their children. And a loving person with godlike powers could simply calm the sea, or grant everyone's bodies the power to resist serious injury, so then the only tragedy they must come together to overcome is temporary pain and the loss of worldly goods. *We* would have done these things, if we could—and God can. Therefore, either God would have done them, too—or God is worse than us. Far worse. Either way, Christianity is false.

The logic of this is again unassailable. So Christians feel compelled to contrive more *ad hoc* excuses to explain away the evidence—more speculations about free will, or "mysterious plans," or a desire to test us or increase opportunities for us to do good, and a whole line of stuff like that. And yet Christians again have no evidence any of these excuses are actually true. They simply "make them up" in order to explain away the failure of their theory. But just as before, even putting that serious problem aside, these *ad hoc* elements *still* fail. For there is no getting around the conjunction of facts entailed by the Christian theory. God cannot possibly struggle under any limitations greater than the limitations upon us (if anything, he must surely have fewer limitations than we do), and God "loves love"—and is therefore a loving being, which means he desires to act like one. These two elements of the hypothesis entail observations, and nothing can explain away the fact that these observations are never made—unless we contradict and therefore reject either of these two essential components of the theory. So the Christian theory is either empirically false, or self-contradictory and therefore *logically* false.

In fact, all the *ad hoc* excuses for God's total and utter inaction amount to the same thing: claiming that different rules apply to God than to us. But this is not allowed by the terms of the theory, which hold that God is good—which must necessarily mean that God is "good" in the same sense that God expects us to be good. Otherwise, calling God "good" means something different than calling anyone else "good," and therefore calling God "good" is essentially meaningless. If God can legitimately be called "good," this must mean exactly the same thing when you or I are called "good." And the fact that God is predicted by the Christian theory to "love love and hate hatred" confirms this conclusion, since "loving love and hating hatred" is exactly what it means to call you or I "good." To be good is to be loving and not hateful. And that entails a certain behavior.

"Love your neighbor as yourself" is universally agreed to mean giving your neighbor what he needs, helping him when he is hurt or in trouble, giving him what he has earned, and taking nothing from him that he has not given you. It means giving water to the thirsty, protecting children from harm, healing infirmities. Jesus himself said so. He did or said all these things, we are told, and the Christian surely must believe this. Therefore, for

23

God to be "good" entails that God must have the desire to do all these things—and there is no possible doubt whether he lacks the *means* to do all these things. And anyone with the means and the desire to act, will act. Therefore, that God does none of these things entails either that he lacks the means or the desire. Once again, either way, Christianity is false.

This conclusion follows because there cannot be any limitation on God greater than the limitations upon us. So God must necessarily desire and have the unimpeded means to do everything you and I can do, and therefore *the Christian God would at least do everything you and I do*. The fact that he doesn't proves he doesn't exist. Therefore, all the excuses invented for God simply don't work. Because it does not matter what plans God may have, he still could not restrain himself from doing good any more than we can, because that is what it means to *be* good. He would be moved by his goodness to act, to do what's right, just as we are. God would not make excuses, for nothing could ever thwart his doing what is morally right.

Hence anything God would refrain from doing can be no different than what any other good people refrain from. Children must learn, often the hard way. But that never in a million years means letting them get hit by a car so they can learn not to cross the road without looking. People must know struggle, so they feel they have earned and learned what matters. But that never in a million years means letting them be tortured or raped or wracked with debilitating disease so they can appreciate being healthy or living in peace. No loving person could ever bear using such cruel methods of teaching, or ever imagine any purpose justifying them. Indeed, a loving person would suffer miserably if he could do nothing to stop such things...or worse, if he actually *caused* them!

Conversely, any excuse that could ever be imagined for God's inaction must necessarily apply to us as well. If there is a good reason for God to do nothing, then it will be just as good a reason for us to do nothing. The same moral rules that are supposed to apply to us must apply to every good person—and that necessarily includes the Christian God. God cannot have more reasons to do nothing than we do—to the contrary, it must be the other way around: only we have limitations on our abilities, creating more legitimate reasons for inaction than can ever apply to God. So if it is good for me to alleviate suffering, it is good for God to do so in those same circumstances. And if it is good for God to refrain from acting, it is good for me to do so in those same circumstances.

Nor can it be argued that God must sit back to give us the chance to do good. For that is not how good people act. Therefore, a "good" God can never have such an excuse. Imagine it. You can heal someone of AIDS. You have the perfect cure sitting in your closet. And you know it. But you do nothing, simply to allow scientists the chance to figure out a cure by themselves—even if it takes so long that billions of people must suffer miserably and die before they get it right. In what world would that *ever* be the right thing to do? In no world at all. When we have every means safely at our disposal, we can only tolerate sitting back to let others do good when others are actually doing good. In other words, if misery is *already* being alleviated, perhaps even at our very urging, then obviously we have nothing left to do ourselves. But it would be unbearable, unconscionable, outright *immoral* to hide the cure for AIDS just to teach everyone a lesson. That is not how a good person could or ever would behave.

This same conclusion follows in many ways. As a friend, I would think it shameful if I didn't give clear, honest advice to my friends when asked, or offer comfort when they are in misery or misfortune. I loan them money when they need it, help them move, keep them company when they are lonely, introduce them to new things I think they'll like, and look out for them. God does none of these things for anyone. Thus he is a friend to none. A man who calls himself a friend but who never speaks plainly to you and is never around when you need him is no friend at all.

And it won't do to say God's with "some" people—speaking to, comforting, and helping them out—because this means he doesn't really love all beings, and is therefore not all-loving. This would make him less decent than even many humans I know. And it's sickeningly patronizing to say, in the midst of misery, loneliness, or need, that "God's with you in spirit," that he pats you on the head and says "There! There!" (though not even in so many words as that). A friend who did so little for us, despite having every resource and ability to do more, and nothing to lose by using them, would be ridiculing us with his disdain. Thus, we cannot rescue the idea of God as Friend to All. The evidence flatly refutes the existence of any such creature. It therefore flatly refutes Christianity.

Likewise, as a loving parent, I would think it a horrible failure on my part if I didn't educate my children well, and supervise them kindly, teaching them how to live safe and well, and warning them of unknown or unexpected dangers. If they *asked* me to butt out I might. But if they didn't, it would be unconscionable to ignore them, to offer them no comfort, protection, or advice. Indeed, society would deem me fit for prison if I did. It would be felony criminal neglect. Yet that is God: An absentee mom—who lets kids get kidnapped and murdered or run over by cars, who does nothing to teach them what they need to know, who never sits down like a loving parent to have an honest chat with them, and who would let them starve if someone else didn't intervene. As this is unconscionable, almost any idea of a god that fits the actual evidence of the world is unconscionable. And any such deity could never be the Christian God. That leaves no way to escape the conclusion: God's inaction alone refutes Christianity.

Wrong Evidence

Besides God's silence and inaction, another reason I am not a Christian is the sheer lack of evidence. Right from the start, Christians can offer no evidence at all for their most important claim, that faith in Jesus Christ procures eternal life. Christians can't point to a single proven case of this prediction coming true. They cannot show a single believer in Jesus actually enjoying eternal life, nor can they demonstrate the probability of such a fortunate outcome arising from any choice we make today. Even if they could prove God exists and created the universe, it still would not follow that belief in Jesus saves us. Even if they could prove Jesus performed miracles, claimed to speak for God, and rose from the dead, it still would not follow that belief in Jesus saves us.

Therefore, such a claim must itself be proven. Christians have yet to do that. We simply have no evidence that any believer ever has or ever will enjoy eternal life, or even that any unbeliever won't. And most Christians agree. As many a good Christian will tell you, *only God knows who will receive his grace.* So the Christian cannot claim to know whether it's true that "faith in Christ procures eternal life." They have to admit there is no guarantee a believer will be saved, or that an unbeliever won't be. God will do whatever he wants. And no one really knows what that is. At best, they propose that faith in Christ will "up your chances," but they have no evidence of even that.

Now, this could change. It is theoretically possible to build a strong circumstantial case that God exists, that he has the means to grant us eternal life, that he never lies, and that he actually did promise to save us if we pledge allegiance to the right holy minion. But that's a lot of extraordinary claims to prove, requiring a lot of extraordinary evidence. Christians simply don't come close to proving them. Of course, Christianity could be reduced to a trivial tautology like "Christ is just an idea, whatever idea brings humankind closer to paradise," but that is certainly not what C.S. Lewis would have accepted, nor is it what most Christians mean today. When we stick with what Christianity usually means, there is simply not enough evidence to support believing it. This holds for the more generic elements of the theory (like the existence of God and the supernatural), as well as the very specific elements (like the divinity and resurrection of Jesus). I shall treat these in order, after digressing on some essential points regarding method.

A Digression on Method

Long ago, people could make up any theories they wanted. As long as their theory fit the evidence, it was thought credible. But an infinite number of incompatible theories can fit the evidence. We can design a zillion religions that fit all the evidence, yet entail Christianity is false. And we can design a zillion secular worldviews that do the same. We could all be brains in a vat. Buddha could have been right. Allah may be the One True God. The universe might have been intelligently designed by a complex alien fungus. And so on, *ad infinitum*. But since only one of these countless theories can be true, it follows that the odds are effectively infinity to one against any theory being true that is *merely* compatible with the evidence. In other words, not a chance in hell. Therefore, we cannot believe a theory simply because it can be made to fit all the evidence. To do so would effectively guarantee our belief will be false.

Fortunately, people came up with what we now call the scientific method, a way to isolate some of these theories compatible with all the evidence and demonstrate that they are more likely to be true than any of the others.[†] The method works

---

[†] I survey the basics of sound method in my book *Sense and Goodness without God* (pp. 49-62 & 213-52). I will soon provide a formal discussion of sound method in *Bayes' Theorem and Historical Method*, but in the meantime you can learn the basics from the experts: E.T. Jaynes & G.L.

like this (and this is very important): first we come up with a hypothesis that explains everything we have so far observed (and this could be nothing more than a creative guess or even a divine revelation—it doesn't matter where a hypothesis comes from); then we deduce what else would have to be observed, and what could never be observed, if that hypothesis really were true (the most crucial step of all); and then we go and look to see if our predictions are fulfilled in practice. The more they are fulfilled, and the more different ways they are fulfilled, the more likely it is that our hypothesis is true.

But that isn't the end of it. To make sure our theories are more likely the true ones (as any old theory can be twisted to fit even this new evidence), they have to be cumulative—which means, compatible with each other and even building on each other—and every element of a theory has to be in evidence. We can't just "make up" anything. Whatever we make up has to be found in the evidence. For example, when Newton explained the organization of the solar system, he knew he was restricted to theories that built on already proven hypotheses. Every element of his theory of the solar system was proved somewhere, somehow:

Bretthorst, *Probability Theory: The Logic of Science* (2003) and Brian Skyrms, *Choice and Chance: An Introduction to Inductive Logic* (4th ed., 1999); Hugh Gauch, Jr., *Scientific Method in Practice* (2002) and Ronald Giere, *Understanding Scientific Reasoning* (1996); and Susan Haack, *Evidence and Inquiry* (1995).

the law of gravity had an independent demonstration, the actual courses of the planets were well observed and charted, and so on. Nothing in his theory was simply "made up" out of whole cloth. He knew the data on planetary behavior had been multiply confirmed. He knew there was gravity acting at a distance. He knew some other things about physics had been proven. The rest followed as a matter of course.

Consider a different analogy. Suppose a man is on trial for murder and, in his own defense, proposes the theory that his fingerprints ended up on the murder weapon because a devious engineer found a way to "copy and paste" his fingerprints, and did so to satisfy a grudge against him. No one on the jury would accept this theory, nor should anyone ever believe it—unless and until the defendant can confirm in evidence every element of the theory. He must present independent evidence that there really is an engineer who really does have the ability to do this sort of thing. He must present independent evidence that this engineer really does hold a grudge against him. And he must present independent evidence that this engineer had the access and opportunity to accomplish this particular trick when and where it had to have happened. Only then does the defendant's theory become even remotely believable—believable enough to create a reasonable doubt that the defendant's fingerprints got there because he touched the weapon.

But to go beyond that, to actually convict this engineer of fixing the evidence like this, *even more* evidence would be necessary—such as independent evidence that he has or had the equipment necessary to pull off this trick, and had used that equipment at or around the time of the crime, and so on. That's how it works. That the "devious engineer's fingerprint trick" fits all the immediate evidence at hand (the existence of the fingerprints on the weapon) is not even a remotely sufficient reason to believe it's true. Rather, every element of the theory must be proved with evidence that is *independent* from the evidence being explained. In other words, the mere existence of the fingerprints on the weapon is not enough evidence that the devious engineer put them there.

Now instead imagine the defendant argued that the fingerprints were placed there by an angel from God. Just think of what kind of evidence he would have to present to prove *that* theory. No less than that would be required to prove any other claim about God's motives and activities, right down to and including the claim that God created the universe or raised Jesus from the dead. This standard is hard to meet precisely because meeting a hard standard is the only way to know you probably have the truth. Otherwise, you are far more likely to be wrong than right.

Therefore, even if it could be contrived to fit all the facts—even the incredible facts of God's absolute silence and complete inactivity in our own experience—the Christian theory is still no better than any other unproven hypothesis in which belief is unwarranted. Belief in Newton's theory would have been unwarranted without evidence supporting the law of gravity, just as belief in the "devious engineer's fingerprint trick" would be unwarranted without any of the required supporting evidence. And Christianity will rightly remain no more credible than this "devious engineer's fingerprint trick" until such time as *every required element of that theory has been independently confirmed by empirical evidence.*

For example, the Christian theory requires that God has a loving character. Therefore, we need at least as much evidence of that entity as we would expect in order to establish the existence of a human being with a loving character. I may tell you there is a man named Michael who is a very good man. But if I build any theory on that premise —like "You should do what Michael says," "Your neighbor could not have been the one who robbed your house, because Michael is your neighbor and he is a very good man," or "Don't worry about losing your job, because there is this man who lives near you named Michael and he is a very good man"—I must first establish that the premise is true: that there is such a man, and that he is in fact very good. Whatever evidence would convince anyone of this fact, will also be sufficient to convince them that there is this guy named God who is a very good person. But the case must still be made. The underlying premise must still be proven. We must have evidence of the existence of this Michael or this God, and evidence that their character is indeed really good, before we can believe *any* theory that requires this particular claim to be true.

If I added further premises, like "Michael has supernatural powers and can conjure gold to support your family," I would have to prove them, too. This goes for God, as well. "He is everywhere." "He is invisible." "He can save your soul." And so on. I cannot credibly assert these things if I cannot prove them from real and reliable evidence. This is a serious problem for the Christian religion as an actual theory capable of test and therefore of warranted belief. None of these things have ever been observed. No one has observed a real act of God, or any real evidence of his inhabiting or observing the universe. So no one has really seen any evidence that he is good, or even exists. Therefore, even after every possible excuse is made for it, the Christian theory is just like all those other theories that merely fit the evidence but have no evidential support, and so it is almost certainly as false as all those other theories. We may as well believe a complex alien fungus created the universe.

In truth, it is even worse for Christianity, since it is not like the proposed "devious engineer's fingerprint trick" but more like the "angel from God forged the fingerprints" theory. And that is a far more serious problem—because the evidence required for *that* kind of claim is far greater than for any other. This, too, is an inescapable point of logic. If I say I own a car, I don't have to present very much evidence to prove it, because you have already observed mountains of evidence that people like me own cars. All of that evidence (for the general proposition "people like him own cars") provides so much support for the particular proposition ("he owns a car") that only minimal evidence is needed to confirm that particular proposition.

But if I say I own a nuclear missile, we are in different territory. You have just as large a mountain of evidence, from your own study as well as direct observation, that "people like him own nuclear missiles" is *not* true. Therefore, I need much more evidence to prove that particular claim—in fact, I need about as much evidence (in quantity and quality) as would be required to prove the general proposition "people like him own nuclear missiles." I don't mean I would have to prove that proposition, but that normally the weight of evidence needed to prove *that* proposition would in turn provide the needed background support for the particular proposition that "I own a nuclear missile," just as it does in the case of "I own a car." So lacking that support, I need to build at least as much support *directly* for the particular proposition "I own a nuclear missile," which means as much support *in kind and degree* as would be required to otherwise prove the general proposition "people like him own nuclear missiles." And that requires a lot of very strong evidence—just as for any general proposition.

We all know this, even if we haven't thought about it or often don't see reason—because this is how we all live our lives. Every time we accept a claim on very little evidence in everyday life, it is usually because we already have a mountain of evidence for one or more of the general propositions that support it. And every time we are skeptical, it is usually because we *lack* that same kind of evidence for the general propositions that would support the claim. And to replace that missing evidence is a considerable challenge.

This is the logical basis of the principle that "extraordinary claims require extraordinary evidence." A simple example is a lottery. The odds of winning a lottery are very low, so you might think it would be an extraordinary claim for me to assert "I won a lottery." But that is not a correct analysis. For lotteries are routinely won. We have observed countless lotteries being won and have tons of evidence that people win lotteries. Therefore, the general proposition "people like him win lotteries" is already well-confirmed, and so I normally don't need very much evidence to convince you that I won a lottery. Of course, I would usually need more evidence for that than I need to prove "I own a car," simply because the number of people who own cars is much greater than the number who win lotteries. But still, the general proposition that "people win lotteries" is amply confirmed. Therefore, "I won a lottery" is not an extraordinary claim. It is, rather, a fairly routine claim—even if not as routine as owning a car.

In contrast, "I own a nuclear missile" would be an extraordinary claim. Yet, even then, you still have a large amount of evidence that nuclear missiles exist, and that at least some people do have access to them. And yet the Department of Homeland Security would still need *a lot* of evidence before it stormed my house looking for one. Now suppose I told you "I own an interstellar spacecraft." That would be an even more extraordinary claim—because there is no general proposition supporting it that is even remotely confirmed. Not only do you have very good evidence that "people like him own interstellar spacecraft" is *not* true, you also have no evidence that this has ever been true for anyone—unlike the nuclear missile. You don't even have reliable evidence that interstellar spacecraft *exist*, much less reside on earth. Therefore, the burden of evidence I would have to bear here is enormous. Just think of what it would take for you to believe me, and you will see what I mean.

Once we appeal to common sense like this, everyone concedes that extraordinary claims require extraordinary evidence. And Christianity quite clearly makes very extraordinary claims: that there is a disembodied, universally-present being with magical powers; that this superbeing actually conjured and fabricated the present universe from nothing; that we have souls that survive the death of our bodies (or that our bodies will be rebuilt in the distant future by this invisible superbeing); and that this being possessed the body of Jesus two thousand years ago, who then performed many supernatural deeds before miraculously rising from the grave to chat with his friends, and then flew up into outer space.

Not a single one of these claims has any proven general proposition to support it. We have never observed any evidence for any "disembodied being" or any person who was present "every-where." We have never observed anyone who had magical powers, or any evidence that such powers even exist in principle (what stories we do have of such people are always too dubious to trust, and always remain unconfirmed in practice). We have no good evidence that we have death-surviving souls or that anyone can or will resurrect our bodies. We have never confirmed that anyone was ever possessed by God. We have never observed anyone performing anything confirmed to be miraculous, much less rising from graves or any comparable ability. Supposed claims of psychic powers, astrological prediction, biblical prophecy, and so on, have all turned out to be unprovable or outright bunk.

Therefore, these are without doubt extraordinary claims every bit as much as "I own an interstellar spacecraft," and indeed are even more extraordinary than *that*. For we already have tons of evidence confirming the elements of the general proposition that "there *can be* an interstellar spacecraft." We could probably build one today with present technology. But we have no evidence whatsoever confirming the general propositions "there can be a disembodied superbeing," "there can be

disembodied souls," "there can be genuine miracles," and so on.

I do not mean these things are not logically
possible. What I mean is that we have no evidence
they are physically possible, much less real, in the
way we know an interstellar spacecraft *is* physically possible or that a nuclear missile *is* real. Therefore, Christianity entails many of the most extraordinary claims conceivable. It therefore requires the most extraordinary amount of evidence
to believe it, even more evidence than would be
needed to believe that I own an interstellar spacecraft. And Christianity simply doesn't come even
remotely close to meeting this standard. It could—
just as I am sure I could prove to you I owned an
interstellar spacecraft, if I actually had one. So I am
sure I could prove to you that Christianity is true...
if it actually were.†

That's the proper way to get at the truth.
Now back to the point...

All the Wrong Evidence

Consider the generic claims that God exists, God is
good, and God created this universe. What evidence do we have for any of these particular propositions? The only evidence ever offered for the "existence" of God essentially boils down to two

---

† For some examples of how I could have done that, see *Sense
and Goodness without God* (pp. 222-52 & 273-75), *The
Christian Delusion* (pp. 307-09), and my chapters in *The End
of Christianity*.

things: "The universe exists, therefore God exists" and "I feel God exists, therefore he does." Otherwise, we can't prove anyone has ever really seen God—seen him act, speak, or do anything (even by some supernatural proxy). Even if we could prove a single genuine miracle had ever really happened, we still would not have evidence that God caused that miracle, rather than a misunderstood human power over the supernatural, or the work of spirits, or sorcery, and so on. To confirm God as their cause would require yet more evidence, of which (again) we have none.

As for those who claim to have "seen" or "spoken" to God, it turns out on close examination (when we even have the required access to find out) that they are lying, insane, or only imagining what they saw or heard. Even believers concede that this is most often the case—because they must, in order to explain all the non-Christian visions and divine communications pervading human history and contemporary world cultures. These always turn out to be subjective experiences "in their minds," and they are rarely consistent with each other. Rather, we find a plethora of contradictory experiences which seem more attenuated to cultural and personal expectations than to anything universally true. Dreams and visions and voices, across all times and sects and world religions and cultures, just don't contain any consistent content —as I explained in my previous chapter on God's silence. If God didn't cause those "other" cases (and you must conclude he didn't, lest you convict

God of being a liar), then you can't claim God caused "your" cases. The same causes are likely at work in both.

So, too, for the "feeling" that God exists. This is no different than the "feeling" I once had that the Tao governs the universe (which I describe in an early section of *Sense and Goodness without God*), or the "feeling" others have had that aliens visit them, the spirits of the dead talk to them, or several gods and nature spirits live all around them. Just like dreams and revelations, people have "felt" the existence of so many contradictory things that we know "feeling" something is the poorest possible evidence we can have. Most people "feel" something completely different than we do, and since there is no way to tell whether your feeling is correct and theirs is wrong, it is just as likely that theirs is correct and yours is wrong. And since there are a million completely different "feelings" and only one can be true, it follows that the odds are worse than a million to one against *your* feeling being the true one. So "feeling" that God exists fails to meet even a minimal standard of evidence, much less an extraordinary standard. And as I said, the very same goes even for more "profound" religious experiences involving the actual appearances or voices of supposedly supernatural beings.[†] So

---

[†] On the known causes and kinds of religious experience across all religions and cultures see: Ilkka Pyysiäinen, *Supernatural Agents: Why We Believe in Souls, Gods, and Buddhas* (2009); Daniel Dennett, *Breaking the Spell: Religion as a Natural Phenomenon* (2006); John Horgan, *Rational Mysticism*

we have no evidence here. As I explained earlier, were the Christian God genuinely communicating with us, his communications would be consistent across all times and regions.

Other than all that, which as demonstrated is simply the wrong evidence to have, people offer the existence of the universe as "proof" that God exists. Some propose that there would be no universe if there wasn't a god, but this is not a logical conclusion. A theory like "nature just exists" is by itself no less likely than "a god just exists." Others propose that since the universe had a beginning, a god must have started it, but this fails both empirically and logically. Empirically, a beginning of time and space became suspect once examination of the quantum theory of gravity led to the realization that a beginning of space-time at a dimensionless point (called a singularity) is actually physically impossible. So now most cosmologists believe there was probably something around before the Big Bang—and probably quite a lot of things (I'll return to this point in the next chapter). As a result, we no longer know if the universe had a beginning.[†] And logically, even if the universe had a beginning, this does not entail or even imply that an

---

(2003); Pascal Boyer, *Religion Explained* (2002); Scott Atran, *In Gods We Trust* (2002); and Stewart Guthrie, *Faces in the Clouds* (1993).

[†] Read: G. Veneziano's article "The Myth of the Beginning of Time" in *Scientific American* 290.5 (2004): pp. 54-65; Paul Davies' article "Multiverse Cosmological Models" in *Modern Physics Letters A* 19:10 (2004): pp. 727-43; and Stephen Hawking's latest book *The Grand Design* (2010).

intelligent being preceded it. If God can exist before the existence of time or space, so could the nature of the universe (as many cosmologists argue, all we would need is a fairly simple quantum state to get everything else going). In short, the appearance of time and space may have simply been an inevitable outcome of the nature of things, just as Christians must believe that God's nature and existence is inevitable. And since it can be either, the mere fact of there being a universe is evidence for neither.

The most popular—and really, the *only* evidence people have for God's existence and role as Creator—is the apparent "fine tuning" of the universe to produce life. That's at least something remarkable, requiring an explanation better than mere chance. As it turns out, there are godless explanations that make more sense of the actual universe we find ourselves in than Christianity does—but we shall examine this point in the next chapter (pp. 66-80). For now, it is enough to point out that "intelligent design" is not the only logically possible explanation for the organization of the universe, either, and so we would need specific empirical evidence for it. Just as scientists needed copious amounts of evidence before justifying a belief that the present cosmos was the inevitable physical outcome of the Big Bang, so do Christians need copious amounts of evidence before justifying a belief that the organization that arose from the Big Bang came from an intelligent engineer. Again, the mere possibility is not enough—we need actual evidence that an intelligent engineer was the cause, and not something else. And Christians don't have that. Or anything like it.

Finally, to prove "God is good" we have essentially nothing at all. Since God is a totally silent do-nothing (as I surveyed in the previous two chapters), we don't have anything to judge his character by, except an utter lack of any clear or consistent action on his part—which we saw earlier is sufficient to demonstrate that if there is a God, he is almost certainly *not* good (and therefore Christianity is false). Christians do try to offer evidence of God's goodness anyway, but what they come up with is always just circular logic or far too weak to meet any reasonable burden.

For example, some argue "God gave us life" as evidence he is good, but that presupposes God is our creator, and so is generally a circular argument. But it also fails to follow from the known facts, since a mindless natural process can also give us life, and even an evil or ambivalent God could have sufficient reason to give us life. Moreover, the harsh kind of life we were given agrees more with *those* possibilities than with the designs of a good God, much less the Christian God, especially since there is as much bad in life as good, and no particular sense of merit in how it gets distributed. In fact, the evidence is even worse for Christianity on this score, since if the universe was intelligently designed, it appears to have been designed for a purpose other than us—but, again, I'll get back to that in the following chapter.

Other Christians try to argue that God is probably good because "God gave his one and only son to save us," but that is again circular—for it already *presumes* that Jesus was his son, that God let him die, and that God did this to accomplish something good for us. Until each one of those propositions is confirmed by independent evidence, there is no way to use this "theory" as if it were "evidence" that God existed or was good. Indeed, that "God gave his one and only son to save us" still fails to follow from the known facts because the same deed could have been performed just as readily for different motives, motives that were not so good.

For example, early Christians tried to explain away the existence of pre-Christian resurrection cults by accusing the Devil of fabricating them to fool mankind and lead us astray. That is a coherent theory that could just as easily explain the entire Christian religion. In other words, Christianity may simply be just one more clever scheme to give a devious God a good laugh. And considering all the evil, misery, and torment that has been caused by the Christian religion—and the fact that God, if he exists, quite obviously gave, or allowed to be given, contradictory and mutually hostile messages to Muslims, Christians, Jews, and Hindus with the inevitable and predictable consequence of furthering human conflict and misery—the theory that "God gave his one and only son to screw us" has even more to commend it than the Christian alternative.[†]

So the supposed evidence that Christians try to offer for God's existence, creative activity, or goodness simply doesn't cut it. It turns out not to be evidence, but theories *about* otherwise ambiguous evidence, theories that themselves remain unproven, and often barely plausible when compared with more obvious alternatives that more readily explain the full range of evidence we have. Therefore, the Christian theory has insufficient support to justify believing it. And this remains so even if Christianity is true. For even if it is true, we *still* don't have enough evidence to *know* it is true. By analogy, even if it were true that Julius Caesar survived an arrow wound to his left thigh in the summer of 49 B.C., the fact that we have no evidence of any such wound entails that we have no reason to believe it occurred. We can only believe what we have evidence enough to prove. And there are plenty of true things that don't make that cut.

So much for the general propositions. None that Christianity depends upon have any adequate support. We may as well believe angels magically frame people for murder by planting fingerprints. But that still leaves us with the more specific propositions that Jesus performed miracles and rose from the dead. Many Christians really do offer the miracles and resurrection of Jesus as evidence that

† On the evil, misery, and torment caused by the Christian religion see: James Haught, *Holy Horrors* (1999) and Helen Ellerbe,*The Dark Side of Christian History* (1995).

ists and that the Christian theory is true. We will set aside the problem that even doing such things would not prove Jesus was God, since other supernatural powers or agencies could have arranged the same result, even if all those things happened. More problematic for Christianity is that we have insufficient evidence any of these things really happened. To understand why, let's consider an imaginary alternative...

Hero Savior of Vietnam

Suppose I told you there was a soldier in the Vietnam War named "Hero Savior" who miraculously calmed storms, healed wounds, conjured food and water out of thin air, and then was blown up by artillery, but appeared again whole and alive three days later, giving instructions to his buddies before flying up into outer space right before their very eyes. Would you believe me? Certainly not. You would ask me to prove it.

So I would give you all the evidence I have. But all I have are some vague war letters by a guy who never really met Hero Savior in person, and a handful of stories written over thirty years later by some guys named Bill, Bob, Carl, and Joe. I don't know for sure who these guys are. I don't even know their last names. There are only unconfirmed rumors that they were or knew some of the war buddies of Hero Savior. They might have written earlier than we think, or later, but no one really knows. No one can find any earlier documentation

48

to confirm their stories, either, or their service during the war, or even find these guys to interview them. So we don't know if they really are who others claim, and we're not even sure these are the guys who actually wrote the stories. You see, the undated pamphlets circulating under their names don't say "by Bill" or "by Bob," but "as told by Bill" and "as told by Bob." Besides all that, we also can't find any record of a Hero Savior serving in the war. He might have been a native guide whose name never made it into official records, but still, none of the historians of the war ever mention him, or his amazing deeds, or even the reports of them that surely would have spread far and wide.

Besides the dubious evidence of these late, uncorroborated, unsourced, and suspicious stories, the best thing I can give you is that war correspondence I mentioned, some letters by an army sergeant actually from the war, who claims he was a skeptic who changed his mind. But he never met or saw Hero in life, and never mentions any of the miracles that Bob, Bill, Carl, and Joe talk about. In fact, the only thing this sergeant ever mentions is "seeing" Hero after his death, though not "in flesh and blood," but in a "revelation." That's it.

This sergeant also claims the spirit of Hero Savior now enables him and some others to "speak in tongues" and "prophecy" and heal some illnesses, but none of this has been confirmed or observed by anyone else on record, and none of it sounds any different than what thousands of other cults and gurus have claimed. So, too, for some unconfirmed reports that some of these believers, even this army sergeant, endured persecution or even died for believing they "saw Hero in a revelation"—a fact no more incredible than the Buddhists who set themselves on fire to protest the Vietnam War, certain they would be reincarnated, or the hundreds of people who voluntarily killed themselves at Jonestown, certain their leader (Jim Jones) was an agent of God.

Okay. I've given you all that evidence. Would you believe me then? Certainly not. No one trusts documents that come decades after the fact by unknown authors, and hardly anyone believes the hundreds of gurus today who claim to see and speak to the spirits of the dead, heal illnesses, and predict the future. Every reasonable person expects and requires extensive corroboration by contemporary documents and confirmed eyewitness accounts. Everyone would expect here at least as much evidence as I'd need to prove I owned a nuclear missile, yet the standard required is actually that of proving I own an interstellar spacecraft—for these are clearly very extraordinary claims, and as we saw above, such claims require extraordinary evidence, as much as would be needed, for example, to convince the United Nations that I had an interstellar spacecraft on my lawn. Yet what we have for this Hero Savior doesn't even count as *ordinary* evidence, much less the extraordinary evidence we really need.

To complete the analogy, many other things would rightly bother us. Little is remarkable about the stories told of Hero Savior, for similar stories apparently have been told of numerous Vietnamese sorcerers and heroes throughout history—and no one believes them, so why should we make an exception for Hero? The documents we have from Bob, Bill, Carl, and Joe have also been tampered with—we've found some cases of forgery and editing in each of their stories by parties unknown, and we aren't sure we've caught it all. Apparently, their stories were used by several different cults to support their causes, and these cults all squabble over the exact details of the right cause, and so tell different stories or interpret the stories differently to serve their own particular agenda. And the earliest version, the one told by Bob, which both Bill and Joe clearly copied, and just added to and edited (and even Carl seems to have done the same, just far more loosely), appears to have been almost entirely constructed out of passages from ancient Vietnamese poems, arranged and altered to tell a story full of symbolic and moral meaning. These and many other problems plague the evidence, leaving it even more suspect than normal.

This Hero Savior analogy entirely parallels the situation for Jesus. Jesus even has the same name: "Christ Jesus" in Hebrew literally means "the messiah and savior." In other words, "Hero Savior." The shady state of the evidence is likewise the same, as documented by Bart Ehrmann in *Jesus Interrupted* (2009) a book I strongly recommend.[†]

[†] See also Bart Ehrman, *The New Testament* (3rd ed., 2003) and *Lost Christianities* (2003); Randel Helms, *Who Wrote the*

And the way the Gospels just emulate and adapt prior stories is discussed by many scholars, including myself in *Not the Impossible Faith* (2009), and I will soon publish a book more directly *On the Historicity of Jesus Christ.*[†]

Every reason we would have not to believe these Hero Savior stories applies to the stories of Jesus, with all the same force. All we have attesting his miracles are letters by a guy (Paul) who never saw Jesus except in private "revelations," and Gospels by unknown authors of unknown date using unknown sources and methods to document wildly unbelievable claims we wouldn't trust from any other religion. So if you agree there would be no good reason to believe these Hero Savior stories, you must also agree there is insufficient reason to believe the Jesus Christ stories. Hence I am not a Christian because the evidence is not good enough. For it is no better than the evidence proposed for Hero Savior, and that falls far short of the burden that would have to be met to confirm the very extraordinary claims surrounding him. I make this case in much fuller detail in chapter eleven of John Loftus' book *The Christian Delusion* (2010).

Gospels? (1997); Richard Pervo, *The Mystery of Acts* (2008); and Robert E. Van Voorst, *Jesus Outside the New Testament* (2000).

[†] In the meantime see: Charles H. Talbert, *What is a Gospel?* (1977); Randel Helms, *Gospel Fictions* (1988); Thomas Brodie, *The Birthing of the New Testament* (2004); Dennis MacDonald, *The Homeric Epics and the Gospel of Mark* (2000) and *Does the New Testament Imitate Homer?* (2003).

And That's the Problem...

Things could have been different. For example, if miracle working was still so routine in the Church that scientists could prove that devout Christians alone could genuinely perform miracles—restoring lost limbs, raising the dead, predicting tsunamis and earthquakes (and actually saving thousands with their timely warnings)—then we would have a well-confirmed generalization that would lend a great deal of support to the Gospel stories, reducing the burden on the Christian to prove those stories true. Likewise, if we had credible documents from educated Roman and Jewish eyewitnesses to the miracles and resurrection of Jesus, and if we had simultaneous records even from China recording appearances of this Jesus to spread the Gospel there just days after his death in Palestine, then the Christian would surely have some solid ground to stand on. And the two together—current proof of regular miracles in the Church, and abundant first-hand documentation from reliable observers among the Jews, Romans, and Chinese—would be full and sufficient evidence to believe the claim that Jesus really did perform miracles and rise from the dead, or at least something comparably remarkable.

But that is not what we have. Not even close. Therefore, I do not have enough evidence to justify believing in Christianity. Again, this could easily be changed, even without the evidence above. If Jesus appeared to me now and answered some of my questions, I would believe. If he often spoke to me and I could perform miracles through his overt blessing, I would believe. If everyone all over the world and throughout history, myself included, had the same religious experience, witnessing no other supernatural being—no other god, no other spirit—other than Jesus, and hearing no other message than the Gospel, I would believe. If we got to observe who makes it into Heaven and who doesn't, and thus could confirm the consequences of belief and unbelief, with the same kind and quantity of evidence as we have for the consequences of driving drunk, I would believe. But we get none of these things, or anything like them.

This is a state of evidence that a "loving" God, who "wanted" us to accept the Gospel and set things right, *would not allow*. Therefore, the absence of this evidence not only leaves Christianity without sufficient evidence to warrant our believing it, but it outright refutes Christianity, because Christianity entails the prediction that God would provide enough evidence to save us, to let us make an informed decision. Since this prediction fails, the theory fails. A loving God would not hide the life preserver he supposedly threw to me, nor would he toss it into a fog, but near to me, where it was plain to see, and he would help me accomplish whatever I needed to reach it and be saved. For that is what I would do for anyone else. And no Christian can believe that I, a mere human infidel, am more fair and loving than their own God. So there is no way to escape this conclusion. Christianity is fully refuted by its own dismal state of evidence.

Wrong Universe

Before now I briefly mentioned that the Christian hypothesis actually predicts a completely different universe than the one we find ourselves in. For a loving God who wanted to create a universe solely to provide a home for human beings, and to bring his plan of salvation to fruition, would never have invented *this* universe, but something quite different. Whereas if there is no God, then the universe we actually observe is exactly the sort of universe we would expect to observe.

In other words, if there is no God then this universe is the only kind of universe we would ever find ourselves in, the only kind that could ever produce intelligent life without any supernatural cause or plan. Hence atheism entails exactly the kind of universe we observe, while the Christian theory predicts almost none of the features of our universe. Instead, any Christian theory of the world predicts the universe should have features that in

55

fact it doesn't, and should lack features that in fact it has. Therefore, naturalism is a better explanation than Christianity of the universe we actually find ourselves in. Since naturalism (rejecting all that is supernatural) is the most plausible form of atheism I know (richardcarrier.info/naturalism.html), this is what I shall mean by "atheism" from here on out. I give a formal demonstration of all this in a chapter of John Loftus' *The End of Christianity* (2011), but here I shall outline enough to make the point. Let's look at a few examples of what I mean.

Origin and Evolution of Life

First, the origin of life. Suppose there is no God. If that is the case, then the origin of life must be a random accident. Christians rightly point out that the appearance of the first living organism is an extremely improbable accident. Of course, so is winning a lottery, and yet lotteries are routinely won. Why? Because the laws of probability entail the odds of winning a lottery depend not just on how unlikely a win is—like, let's say, a one in a billion chance—but on how often the game is played. In other words, if a billion people play, and the odds of winning are one in a billion, it's actually highly *probable* that someone will win the lottery. Now, if the game is played only once, and the only ticket sold just happens to be the winner, then you might get suspicious. And if the game was played a billion times, and each time only one ticket was sold and yet every single time it was that ticket that happened to be the winner, then you would be quite certain someone was cheating. For nothing else could easily explain such a remarkable fact.

Therefore, the only way life could arise by accident (i.e. without God arranging it) is if there were countless more failed tries than actual successes. After all, if the lottery was played by a billion people and yet only one of them won, that would surely be a mere accident, not evidence of cheating. So the only way this lottery could be won by accident is if it was played countless times and only one ticket won. To carry the analogy over, the only way life could arise by accident is if the universe tried countless times and only very rarely succeeded. Lo and behold, we observe that is exactly what happened: the universe has been mixing chemicals for over twelve billion years in over a billion-trillion star systems. That is exactly what we would have to see if life arose by accident—because life can *only* arise by accident in a universe as large and old as ours. The fact that we observe exactly what the theory of accidental origin requires and predicts is evidence that our theory is correct.

Of course, we haven't yet proven any particular theory of life's origin true. But we do have evidence for every element of every theory now considered. Nothing about contemporary hypotheses of life's origin rests on any conjecture or assumption that has not been observed or demonstrated in some circumstance. For example, we know porous rocks that can provide a cell-like home were available near energy-rich, deep-sea volcanic vents. We know those vents harbor some of the most ancient life on the planet, indicating that life may well have begun there. And we know these vents would have provided all the necessary resources to produce an amino-acid-based life, and that they had hundreds of millions of years of time in which to do so. In a similar way, we have evidence supporting every other presently viable theory: we know homochiral amino acids can be mass-produced in a supernova and thus become a component of the early comets that bombarded the early Earth; we know that amino acids that chain along a common crystalline structure in clay will chain in a homochiral structure; we know simple self-replicating chains of amino acids exist that do not require any enzymes working in concert; and so on.[†]

So by the rules of sound procedure, the accidental theory is well-grounded in a way intelligent design theory is not. We have never observed or

_____

[†] For current science on the origin of life see: Richard Carrier, "The Argument from Biogenesis: Probabilities Against a Natural Origin of Life," *Biology and Philosophy* 19.5 (November 2004): pp. 739-64; Geoffrey Zubay, *Origins of Life* (2nd ed., 2000); Tom Fenchel, *Origin and Early Evolution of Life* (2003); Andri Brack, *The Molecular Origins of Life* (1998); Noam Lahav, *Biogenesis* (1998); Iris Fry, *The Emergence of Life on Earth* (2000); Christopher Wills & Jeffrey Bada, *The Spark of Life* (2000); J. William Schopf, *Life's Origin* (2002); John Maynard Smith & Eors Szathmary, *The Origins of Life* (1999); and Peter Ward & Donald Brownlee, *Rare Earth* (2000).

confirmed the existence of any sort of divine actions or powers that God would have needed to "create" the first life—nor have we demonstrated the existence of any such agent, not even indirectly (as we have for all the natural theories of life's origin). So the intelligent design theory is completely *ad hoc*, in exactly the way our accidental theory is not, and is therefore not presently credible.

The situation is even worse than that, really. For the Christian theory does not predict what we observe, while the natural theory *does* predict what we observe. After all, what need does an intelligent engineer have of billions of years and trillions of galaxies filled with billions of stars apiece? That tremendous waste is *only* needed if life had to arise by natural accident. It would have no plausible purpose in the Christian God's plan. You cannot predict from "the Christian God created the world" that "the world" would be trillions of galaxies large and billions of years old before it finally stumbled on one rare occasion of life. But we *can* predict exactly that from "no God created this world." Because if there is no God, then life could have arisen *only* in a world that large and old. So that would be the only world we would ever see around us. And lo and behold, that's exactly the world we see around us.

Therefore, the facts confirm atheism rather than theism. Obviously, a Christian can invent all manner of additional *ad hoc* theories to explain "why" his God would go to all the trouble of designing the universe to look exactly like we would expect it to look if God did not exist. But these *ad hoc* excuses are themselves pure concoctions of the imagination. Until the Christian can *prove* these additional theories are true, from independent evidence, there is no reason to believe them, and hence no reason to believe the Christian theory.

The same analysis follows for evolution. The evidence that all present life evolved by a process of natural selection is strong and extensive. I won't repeat the case here, for it is enough to point out that the scientific consensus on this is vast and certain, so if you deny it you're only kicking against the goad of your own ignorance.[†] And as it happens, evolution *requires* billions of years to get all the way from the first accidental life to organisms as complex as us. God does not require this—nor does taking so long make much sense for God, unless he wanted to deliberately fabricate evidence against his existence by planting all the evidence for evolution—all the fossils, all the DNA correlations, the vast scales of time over which changes

---

[†] Besides my summary and bibliography in *Sense and Goodness without God* (pp. 165-76), experts have produced many superb books demonstrating evolution theory is true: Richard Dawkins, *The Greatest Show on Earth* (2009); Jerry Coyne, *Why Evolution Is True* (2009); Donald Prothero, *Evolution: What the Fossils Say and Why It Matters* (2007); Sean Carroll, *The Making of the Fittest: DNA and the Ultimate Forensic Record of Evolution* (2006); Eugenie Scott, *Evolution vs. Creationism* (2004); Ernst Mayr, *What Evolution Is* (2001); Douglas Futuyma, *Science on Trial: The Case for Evolution* (1995).

occurred, everything. Again, there is no credible reason to believe the Christian God would do this, and no actual evidence that he did. It would make him a liar in any case, which by definition the Christian God cannot be, as a "lover of love" would hardly be the prince of lies. In contrast, the only way we could exist *without* God is if we lived at the end of billions of years of meandering change over time. Lo and behold, that is exactly where we observe ourselves to be. Thus, atheism predicts the evidence for evolution, including the vast time involved and all the meandering progress of change in the fossil record, whereas Christian theism does not predict any of this—without adding all manner of undemonstrated *ad hoc* assumptions, assumptions the atheist theory does not require.

Even DNA confirms atheism over Christianity. The only way life could ever arise by accident and evolve by natural selection is if it was built from a chemical code that could be copied and that was subject to mutation. We know of no other natural, accidental way for any universe to just "stumble upon" any kind of life that could naturally evolve. Also, as best we know, the only chemicals that our present universe could accidentally assemble this way are amino acids and related molecules like nucleotides. And it is highly improbable that an accidentally assembled code would employ any more than a handful of basic units in its fundamental structure. Lo and behold, we observe all of this to be the case. Exactly as required by the theory that there is no God, all life is built from a chemical code that copies itself and mutates naturally, this code is constructed from amino-acid-forming nucleotide molecules, and the most advanced DNA code we have only employs four different nucleotide molecules to do that. The Christian theory predicts none of this. Atheism predicts all of it. There is no good reason God would need *any* of these things to create and sustain life. He could, and almost certainly would, use an infallible spiritual essence to accomplish the same ends—exactly as all Christians thought for nearly two thousand years. Instead, we have fallible and malfunctioning DNA that mutates regularly (in life, causing cancer; in reproduction, causing death, disability, or unplanned novelty).

Again, the only way a Christian can explain the actual facts is by pulling out of thin air some unproven "reason" why God would design life in exactly the way required by the theory that life *wasn't* designed by God—a way that was demonstrably inferior to what he could have done. Either God must have a deliberate intent to deceive, which no "good" or "loving" God who "wanted" us to know the truth would ever have, or God has some other motive that just "happens" to entail, by some truly incredible coincidence, doing exactly the same thing as deceiving us into thinking he doesn't exist, which at the same time just "happens" to require adding needless imperfections in our construction. In the one case, Christianity is refuted, and in the other it becomes too incredible to believe—unless the Christian can prove from actual evidence that this coincidental reason really does exist and really has guided God's actions in choosing how to design life and the universe it resides in. The possibility is not enough. You have to prove it. That has yet to happen.

We can find more examples from the nature of life. For example, a loving God would infuse his creation with models of moral goodness everywhere, in the very function and organization of nature. He would not create an animal kingdom that depended on wanton rape and murder to persist and thrive, nor would animals have to produce hundreds of offspring because almost all of them will die, most of them horribly. There would be no disease or other forms of suffering among animals at all. Yet all of these things must necessarily exist if there is no God. So once again, atheism predicts what we see. Christianity does not.

The Human Brain

As a more specific example, consider the size of the human brain. If God exists, then it necessarily follows that a fully functional mind can exist without a body—and if that is true, God would have no reason to give us brains. We would not need them. For being minds like him, being "made in his image," our souls could do all the work, and control our thoughts and bodies directly. At most a very minimal brain would be needed to provide interaction between the senses, nerves, and soul. A brain no larger than that of a monkey would be sufficient, since a monkey can see, hear, smell, and do pretty much everything we can, and its tiny brain is apparently adequate to the task. And had God done that—had he given us real souls that actually perform all the tasks of consciousness (seeing, feeling, thinking)—that would indeed count as evidence for his existence, and against mere atheism.

In contrast, if a mind can *only* be produced by a comparably complex machine, then obviously there can be no God (there being no complex machine to produce him), *and* the human brain would have to be very large—large enough to contain and produce a complex machine like a mind. Lo and behold, the human brain is indeed large—so large that it kills many mothers during labor (without scientific medicine, the rate of mortality varies around 10% per child).[†] This huge brain also consumes a large amount of oxygen and other resources, and it is very delicate and easily damaged. Moreover, damage to the brain profoundly harms a

---

† In ancient times the mortality rate for mothers giving birth varied between 5% and 15% (or from roughly 1 in 20 to 1 in 7): Bernardo Arriaza, et al., "Maternal Mortality in Pre-Columbian Indians of Arica, Chile," *American Journal of Physical Anthropology* 77 (1988): pp. 35-41. From the dawn of the scientific and industrial revolutions, however, things improved, and mortality varied between 0.3% and 8% (from roughly 1 in 300 to 1 in 12), until the early 20th century, when it began to decline in most nations to the point that fewer than one in several thousand women die because of childbirth (except in the poorest of countries): Irvine Louden, "Deaths in Childbed from the Eighteenth Century to 1935," *Medical History* 30 (1986): pp. 1-41.

human's ability to perceive and think. So our large brain is a considerable handicap, the cause of needless misery and death and pointless inefficiency—which is not anything a loving engineer would give us, nor anything a good or talented engineer with godlike resources would ever settle on.

But this enormous, problematic brain is necessarily the *only* way conscious beings can exist if there is no God (nor any other supernatural powers in the universe). If we didn't need a brain, and thus did not have one, we would be many times more efficient. All that oxygen, energy, and other materials could be saved or diverted to other functions (we would need less air to breathe, less food to eat). We would also be far less vulnerable to fatal or debilitating injury. We would be immune to brain damage, and defects that impair judgment or distort perception (like schizophrenia or retardation), and we wouldn't have killed one in every ten of our mothers before the rise of medicine. In short, the fact that we have such large, vulnerable brains is the only way we could exist if there is no God, but is quite improbable if there is a God who loves us and wants us to do well and have a fair chance in life. Once again, when it comes to our brains, atheism predicts the universe we find ourselves in. The Christian theory does not.[†]

---

† Experts are all agreed on the physical, brain-dependent nature of our minds: David Linden, *The Accidental Mind* (2007), Joseph Ledoux, *Synaptic Self* (2002), and William Libaw, *How We Got to Be Human* (2000); plus: Gary Marcus, *Kluge: The Haphazard Construction of the Human Mind* (2008);

Finely Tuning a Killer Cosmos

Even the Christian proposal that God designed the universe, indeed "finely tuned" it to be the perfect mechanism for producing life, fails to predict the universe we see. A universe perfectly designed for life would easily, readily, and abundantly produce and sustain it. Most of the contents of that universe would be conducive to life or benefit life. Yet that is not what we see. Instead, almost the entire universe is lethal to life—in fact, if we put all the lethal vacuum of outer space swamped with deadly radiation into an area the size of a house, you would never find the submicroscopic speck of area that sustains life. It would be smaller than a single proton. Would you conclude that the house was built to serve and benefit that subatomic speck? Hardly. Yet that is the house we live in. The Christian theory completely fails to predict this. But atheism predicts exactly this.

The fact that the universe is actually very poorly designed to sustain and benefit life is already a refutation of the Christian theory, which entails the purpose of the universe is to sustain and benefit life—human life in particular. When we

---

Gerald Edelman, *Wider than the Sky* (2004); Steven Johnson, *Mind Wide Open* (2004); Christof Koch, *The Quest for Consciousness* (2004); Susan Blackmore, *Consciousness: An Introduction* (2003); Robert Aunger, *The Electric Meme* (2002); and V.S. Ramachandran, *Brief Tour of Human Consciousness* (2004) and*Phantoms in the Brain* (1999).

look at how the universe is actually built, we do find that it appears perfectly designed after all—but not for producing life. Lee Smolin has argued from the available scientific facts that our universe is probably the most perfect universe that could ever be arranged *for producing black holes.*[†] He also explains how all the elements that would be required to finely tune a perfect black-hole-maker also make chemical life like ours an extremely rare but inevitable byproduct of such a universe. This means that if the universe was designed, it was not designed to make and sustain *us*, but to make and sustain black

---

[†] Lee Smolin, "Did the Universe Evolve?" *Classical and Quantum Gravity* 9 (1992): pp. 173-192; Damien Easson & Robert Brandenberger, "Universe Generation from Black Hole Interiors," *Journal of High Energy Physics* 6.24 (2001). In light of John Barrow's demonstration that the precise dimensionality of our universe is also optimal for life (John Barrow, "Dimensionality," *Philosophical Transactions of the Royal Society of London: Series A, Mathematical and Physical Sciences* 310.1512, December 1983: pp. 337-46), which happens also to demonstrate the same optimality for black hole formation as Smolin proposes, support for Smolin's theory is thus provided by the plausible link made, by superstring theory, between dimensionality and the numbers and properties of all subatomic particles: i.e. if a specific dimensionality entails a precise set of particles, then Smolin's demonstration that our precise set is optimal for black hole formation entails that our universe's specific dimensionality is likewise optimal for black hole formation (when we consider that Barrow's discussion does not exclude the addition of the collapsed dimensions required by string theory). See: John Gribbin, *The Search for Superstrings, Symmetry, and the Theory of Everything* (2000); L.E. Lewis, Jr., *Our Superstring Universe* (2003); and Brian Greene,*The Fabric of the Cosmos* (2004).

holes, and therefore even if there is a God he cannot be the Christian God. Therefore, even on a *successful* fine-tuning argument Christianity is false.

Smolin explains how a universe perfectly designed to produce black holes would look exactly like our universe. It would be extremely old, extremely large, and almost entirely comprised of radiation-filled vacuum, in which almost all the matter available would be devoted to producing black holes or providing the material that feeds them. We know there must be, in fact, billions more black holes than life-producing planets. And if any of several physical constants varied by even the tiniest amount, the universe would produce fewer black holes—hence these constants have been arranged into the perfect combination for producing the most black holes possible. The number and variety and exact properties of subatomic particles has the same effect—any difference, and our universe would produce fewer black holes.

Christianity predicts none of these things. What use does God have for quarks, neutrinos, muons, or kaons? They are necessary only if God wanted to build a universe that was a perfect black hole generator. This is so even if the correlation is a coincidence: if only perfect black-hole generators can accidentally produce life, then atheism predicts exactly the universe we observe, whereas God has no need of complex systems of physical constants and subatomic particles to create a place for life. Do you really think everything in heaven is also made of photons, gluons and quarks and subject to

the strong nuclear force and radioactive decay?
Worse, do you really think God is so powerless he
couldn't build a world *except* with photons, gluons
and quarks and the strong nuclear force and radioactive decay? (Not even heaven?) Surely God has
no need of such things.

Think about it. If you found a pair of scissors
and didn't know what they were designed for, you
could hypothesize they were designed as a screw-
driver, because scissors can, after all, drive screws.
In fact, there is no way to design a pair of scissors
that would prevent them being used as a screw-
driver. But as soon as someone showed you that
these scissors were far better designed to cut paper,
and in fact are not the best design for driving
screws, would you stubbornly hang on to your theory that they were designed to drive screws? No.
You would realize it was obvious they were designed to cut paper, and their ability to drive screws
is just an inevitable byproduct of their actual
design. This is exactly what we are facing when we
look at the universe: it is not very well designed for
life, though life is an inevitable byproduct of what
the universe was more obviously designed for:
black holes. So if the universe was intelligently designed, it clearly was not designed for us.

But that is not the only explanation. If the
universe was indeed perfectly designed to sustain
and benefit life—if the whole cosmos was hospitable and beneficial—*that* would be evidence it was
intelligently or supernaturally designed, since only
an intelligent or supernatural being would ever

have such a goal in mind. But this does not follow for black holes. Smolin explains why. Black holes possess all the same properties that our own Big Bang world possessed before expanding into the present cosmos, so it seems likely that *every* black hole might produce a universe inside it. Smolin then demonstrates that if every black hole produces a new universe slightly different than its parent, then our universe is the inevitable outcome of literally any possible universe that could arise at random. If any universe emerges randomly from a primordial chaos, no matter what arrangement of particles and physical constants that universe accidentally ends up with, it will always produce at least one black hole (even if only by collapsing in on itself), which in Smolin's theory will reset the whole slate, producing an entirely new universe with a newly randomized set of properties. This new universe will in turn produce at least one more black hole, and therefore one more roll of the dice, and on and on, forever. There is nothing that could ever stop this from continuing on to infinity.

Some of these early random universes will just by chance have properties that produce more black holes than other universes, and will thus produce far more baby universes than their cousins do. The more black holes a universe produces, the more likely it is that some of the new universes this causes will also be good at making black holes, or even better. And eventually this chain of cause and effect will generate perfect or near-perfect black hole producers, after an extended and inevitable process of trial and error. Therefore, if the whole multiverse began with any random universe from some primordial chaos—which would always either collapse or rip apart, either way generating at least one new black hole, if not many, and thus inevitably just creating new random universes over and over again—eventually a universe exactly like ours would be an inevitable and unstoppable outcome. Hence Smolin's theory predicts exactly our universe, with all its finely tuned attributes, without any God or intelligent design at all.

Now, Smolin's theory has yet to be proven. It is at present just a hypothesis—but so is Christianity. Just like Christianity, there are elements to Smolin's theory that are conjectural and not independently proven to exist. However, the most important element—the fact that unintelligent natural selection can produce incredibly precise fine tuning over time—*has* been proven, whereas any sort of divine activity has not. We have never observed a single proven case of a god causing anything, much less any fine-tuning of the properties of our universe. But we have found overwhelming evidence for a process that produces very amazing fine-tuning without any intelligence behind it, and that is evolution by natural selection. This is a known precedent—unlike bodiless minds or divine causation. And a theory based on known precedents is always less *ad hoc* than a theory based on completely novel and unobserved mechanisms. So Smolin's theory already has an edge over creationism.

Even so, there are still some *ad hoc* elements to Smolin's theory, and therefore it is not yet a fact, just a hypothesis. But suppose for a moment that Smolin's theory is the only possible way our universe could come to exist without a God. It is certainly one possible way. No Christian can yet refute Smolin's theory or prove it is not the correct explanation. There are also other theories now that explain our exact universe without a God, like chaotic inflation theory. But let's assume we ruled out all those alternatives, and all we had left was Smolin's theory and the Christian's theory. Then, if Christianity was false, Smolin's theory would necessarily be true.

Now observe the facts: the universe is *exactly* the way Smolin's theory predicts it would be, right down to peculiar details—such as the existence and properties of obscure subatomic particles, and the fact that the universe is almost entirely devoted to producing and feeding black holes, is almost entirely inhospitable to life, and almost never produces life. Christianity predicts none of these things, and in fact many of these details are quite improbable if Christianity is true. In contrast, atheism would predict every single one of those details, exactly as we observe. Once again, Christianity predicts a different universe than the one we have —while atheism predicts *exactly* the universe we have. This even extends to the Big Bang theory itself. In no way does Christianity predict God would "create" a universe with a long deterministic process from a gigantic Big Bang. But if Smolin's theory is the only possible explanation of our universe without God, then it necessarily follows that our universe *must* have begun with a Big Bang and evolved slowly over many eons. Yet again, atheism predicts a Big Bang universe. Christianity does not.

Since Smolin's theory makes all this evidence far more likely than Christianity does (indeed Christianity doesn't make any of that evidence even likely at all), if Smolin's theory were shown to be less likely than some *other* godless theory (like chaotic inflation theory, or anything else), then Christianity would be even *more* refuted. Because if Christianity is less likely than Smolin's theory, then Christianity will be even *less* likely than any theory more likely than Smolin's. So the evidence of cosmic and fundamental physics completely refutes Christianity. If Christianity were true, we would have observed a completely different cosmic and physical structure in the world. Instead we see exactly the cosmic and physical structure that must exist *if there is no God*. That can hardly be a coincidence.

Even aside from physics, the nature of the world is clearly dispassionate and blind, exhibiting no value-laden behavior or message of any kind. And everything we find turns out to be the inevitable product of mindless physics. The natural world is like an autistic idiot savant, a marvelous machine wholly uncomprehending of itself or others. This is exactly what we should expect if it was not created and governed by a benevolent deity. Yet it is hardly explicable on the theory that there is

73

such a being. Since there is no observable divine
hand in nature as a causal process, it is reasonable
to conclude there is no divine hand. Conversely, all
the causes whose existence we have confirmed are
unintelligent, immutable forces and objects. Never
once have we confirmed the existence of any other
kind of cause. And that is strange if there is a God,
but not at all strange if there isn't one. Nowhere do
we find in the design of the universe itself any sort
of intention or goal we can only expect from a conscious being like us, as opposed to the sort of goals
exhibited by, say, a flat worm, a computer game, or
an ant colony, or an intricate machine like the solar
system, which simply follows inevitably from natural forces that are fixed and blind.

Given the lack of any clear evidence for God,
and the fact that (apart from what humans do)
everything we've seen has been caused by immutable natural elements and forces, we should sooner
infer that immutable natural elements and forces
are behind it all. Likewise, the only things we have
ever proven to exist are matter, energy, space, and
time, and countless different arrangements and behaviors of these. Therefore, the natural inference is
that these are the only things there are. After all,
the universe exhibits no values in its own operation
or design. It operates exactly the same for everyone, the good and bad alike. It rewards and craps
on both with total disregard. It behaves just like a
cold and indifferent machine, not the creation of a
loving engineer. Christianity does not predict this.
Atheism does. Christianity is therefore refuted.

The *Original* Christian Cosmos

A Christian might still balk and ask, "Well, what other universe could God have made?" The answer is easy: the very universe early Christians like the Apostle Paul actually believed they lived in. In other words, a universe with no evidence of such a vast age or of natural evolution, a universe that contained instead abundant evidence that it was created all at once just thousands of years ago. A universe that wasn't so enormous, and that had no other star systems or galaxies, but was instead a single cosmos of seven planetary bodies and a single sphere of starlights, that all revolve around a single Earth at the center of God's creation—obviously, because that Earth is the center of God's love and attention. A complete cosmos whose marvelously intricate motions had no other explanation than God's will, rather than a solar system whose intricate motions are entirely the inevitable outcome of fixed and blind forces. A universe comprised of five basic elements, not over ninety elements, each in turn constructed from a dizzying array of subatomic particles (we've discovered several dozen different varieties). A universe governed by God's law, not a thoroughly amoral physics. A universe inhabited by animals and spirits whose activity could be confirmed everywhere, and who lived in and descended from outer space—which was not a vacuum, but literally the ethereal heavens, the hospitable home of countless of God's most marvelous creatures (both above and below the Moon)—a place Paul believed human beings could live, and had actually visited without harm (without need of space suits or fear of solar or cosmic radiation, or meteoroids or lethal cold).

That is, indeed, exactly the universe we would expect if Christianity were true—which is why Christianity was contrived as it was, when it was. The first Christians truly believed the universe was exactly as Christian theism predicted it to be, and took that as confirmation of their theory. Lo and behold, they were wrong—about almost every single detail! Paul truly believed that the perfect order of the heavens, the apparent design of human and animal bodies, and the perfect march of the seasons had no other explanation than intelligent design, and in fact he believed in God largely because of this, and condemned unbelievers precisely because they rejected this evidence (Romans 1:18-22).[†] But it turns out none of this evidence really

---

† This ancient view of the cosmos and intelligent design can be found in Galen's extensive demonstration from human anatomy in *On the Use of the Body's Parts*, Ptolemy's *Almagest*, Aristotle's *On the Heavens*, and Plato's extensive cosmology in the *Timaeus*, which became his most popular and influential book, as one can see from reading the works of the Greek scholar Plutarch (e.g. *On Isis and Osiris*) or the Jewish philosopher Philo (e.g. *On the Creation of the Cosmos According to Moses*). A detailed example of how Christians thought the universe was designed can be found in the surviving section of Dionysius of Alexandria's 3rd century treatise *On Nature*. See also Rosemary Wright, *Cosmology in Antiquity* (1995) and Sam Sambursky, *The Physical World of Late Antiquity* (1962).

existed. Christians have long abandoned their belief that the perfect order of the heavens (the movement and placement of the stars and planets) can only be explained by God, since they now know it is entirely explained by physics and requires no intelligent meddling or design. And a great many Christians have abandoned their belief that the apparent design of human and animal bodies can only be explained by God, since they now know it is entirely explicable by natural evolution.

All the evidence we now have only compounds Paul's error. For what we know today is exactly the opposite of what Paul would have expected. It is exactly the opposite of what his Christian theory predicted. Paul certainly would have told you that God would never use billions of years of meandering and disastrously catastrophic trial and error to figure out how to make a human. God would just make humans. And Paul certainly believed that is exactly what God did, and surely expected the evidence would prove it. But the evidence has not. It has, in fact, proved exactly the opposite. Likewise, Paul naturally believed God simply spoke a word, and Earth existed. One more word, and the stars existed. That's exactly what the Christian theory predicts. But that isn't what happened.

Again, Christians can fabricate excuses for why God did things differently than we should expect (and the original Christians did expect)—but that's all just *ad hoc*. Like Christianity, none of these excuses have been demonstrated to be true. It is even doubtful such excuses would be compatible with Christianity. As noted earlier, God can do essentially anything, so what he does is pretty much limited only by what he wants to do. Christianity says he wants us to be good and set things right, which entails that God wants us to know what is good and how to set things right. Christianity says God wants to do what is good, and his choices are guided by his love of love and his hatred of hatred —therefore anything he designed would be the good and admirable product of a loving being. There is no way to "define away" these conclusions. If any of these conclusions are false, Christianity is false. But these conclusions entail that certain things would be true about our universe that are not in fact true.

The existence of a divine creator driven by a mission to save humankind, for example, entails that his creation would serve exactly that end, better than any other. And that means he would not design the universe to look exactly like it would have to look if God did not exist. Instead, if I wanted people to know which church was teaching the right way to salvation, I would lead the way for them by protecting all such churches with mysterious energy fields so they would be invulnerable to harm, and its preachers alone would be able to work miracles day after day, such as regenerating lost limbs, raising the dead, or calming storms. The bibles of this church would glow in the dark so they could always be read and would be indestructible—immune to any attempt to mark, burn, or tear them, or change what they said (and as God I could prevent people from abusing these properties—like making suits of armor out of bibles—in the very way ancient believers thought God did: by visiting humorous but annoying curses on such people until they behaved more reverently). Indeed, I would regard it as my moral obligation to do things like this, so my children would not be in the dark about who I was and what I was about, so they would be able to find out for sure what was truly good for them.

So, too, the Christian God would design a universe with moral goals built in. For example, if I were to make a universe, and cared how the people in it felt—whether they suffered or were happy—I would make it a law of nature that the more good a person really was (not pretended at being), the more invulnerable they would be to harm or illness; and the more evil, the weaker and more ill. Nature would be governed by survival of the kindest, not survival of the fittest. Obviously, such a law would not be possible unless the universe "knew" what good and evil was, and cared about the one flourishing rather than the other. And unlike mere survival, which does its own choosing through the callous mechanism of death, if the very laws of the universe served a highly abstract good instead, that would be inconceivable without a higher mind capable of grasping and caring about all these deep abstract principles—as we know humans do, and the universe does not. So a physical law like this would indeed provide good evidence the universe was created by a loving God.

But, lo and behold, that is not the universe we live in. Even if a God made this universe, it could not be the Christian God because no God who wanted us to know the truth would conceal it by making a universe that looked exactly like a universe with no God in it. The simple fact is that Christianity does not predict our universe, but a completely different one. Atheism, however, predicts *exactly* the kind of universe we find ourselves in. So the nature of the universe is another failed prediction, confirming our previous conclusion that Christianity is false. And like the three others, there isn't any way to escape this conclusion.

Conclusion

As I've clearly shown, Christianity entails that
God, like any other person, would say and do at
least *some* things we would all observe, and we'd
all agree on what they were. Any Christian God
would make sure of that. Since we haven't seen
such things, none at all, the Christian theory of the
world is falsified by the evidence—conclusively.
Christianity also entails that God would have made
the universe very differently than we observe it to
be. It's instead exactly as we'd expect it to appear
if there is no god at all. So again Christianity is
falsified by the evidence—conclusively.

A failed prediction means a failed theory,
especially when these failures apply to the very
nature and design of the universe itself. There is
also insufficient evidence for any of the essential
propositions of Christianity. The evidence offered
doesn't even come remotely close to what common
sense requires, and certainly nowhere near what
you would accept as sufficient to convince you to
adopt any *other* religion. So the Christian hypothesis flatly contradicts a ton of evidence, makes

numerous failed predictions, is not the best explanation of the universe we find ourselves in, and fails to find anywhere near sufficient evidence in its own support. That's more than enough reason to reach my conclusion. Christianity is simply false.

But what do we do then? What do we believe? I answer that question in my book *Sense and Goodness without God*. You can read that for the whole of story, but I can brief it here. Since this world isn't the way we'd want it to be, we have to *make* it the way we want it to be. This world isn't protected by any supreme justice or caregiver, there is no infallible wise man to turn to, no divine hero to love us, and we aren't going to live forever. So *we* have to create those things. We have to create justice, and care for each other and the world we live in. We have to find and give and receive love from each other. We have to be the hero. We have to give our lives meaning. We have to protect life, and invent technologies of immortality—metaphorically (in the way people's words and actions live on in their consequences and memorials), and literally (through medicine, and the science of life extension and resurrection). And until we invent any real immortality, we have to accept the way things are and make the best of the short lives we have. We have to love life rather than fear death. We have to respect life rather than treat it as disposable.

We have to do all of these things. Because that is the world we want to live in—and no one else is going to do any of this for us.

Conclusion

Bibliography for Further Reading

Richard Carrier, *Sense and Goodness without God: A Defense of Metaphysical Naturalism* (Author-House 2005)

Richard Carrier, *Not the Impossible Faith: Why Christianity Didn't Need a Miracle to Succeed* (Lulu 2009)

John Loftus, ed., *The Christian Delusion: Why Faith Fails* (Prometheus 2010)

John Loftus, ed., *The End of Christianity* (Prometheus 2011).

Malcolm Murray, *The Atheist's Primer* (Broadview 2010).

Bart Ehrman, *Jesus Interrupted: Revealing the Hidden Contradictions in the Bible (and Why We Don't Know about Them)* (HarperOne 2009).

Israel Finkelstein & Neil Silberman, *The Bible Unearthed: Archaeology's New Vision of Ancient Israel and the Origin of Its Sacred Texts* (Free Press 2001).

www.richardcarrier.info

Made in the USA
San Bernardino, CA
27 January 2013